REBECCA CLARKE

PASSACAGLIA
on an Old English Tune

(Violoncello and Piano)

ED 4111

ISBN 978-0-634-00566-4

G. SCHIRMER, Inc.

DISTRIBUTED BY

HAL•LEONARD®
CORPORATION

To BB

Passacaglia
on an Old English Tune*

Rebecca Clarke

* Attributed to Thomas Tallis

† The score shows only the Viola part. There are some modifications to the Violoncello part that do not appear in the score.

To BB

Passacaglia
on an Old English Tune

Violoncello

Rebecca Clarke

Violoncello

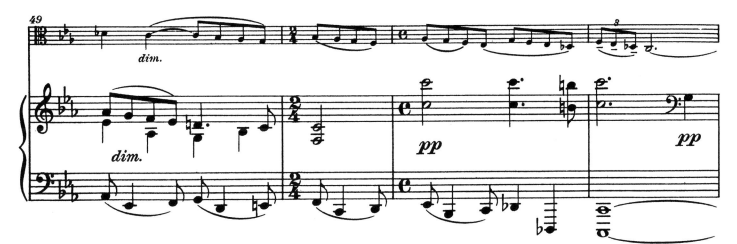

U.S.$9.99

HL50483592

G. SCHIRMER, Inc.

DISTRIBUTED BY

ISBN 978-0-634-00566-4